Introduction:

This booklet contains a full practice exam, written to provide you with the practice experience needed to prepare for the actual exam. This practice exam should help you see whether you have not only memorized your study material but are also able to apply it, which is the only way to pass the exam.

There are 90 questions, distributed over 18 cases. The score to aim for is 80% correct, meaning 18 mistakes or fewer. If you scored 80% or higher, consider yourself ready for exam day.

How to take this practice exam:

Take a piece of paper, a pencil, and a timer. Set the timer for 2.5 hours (although there is more reading during this practice exam compared to the actual exam). Write down the number of the question and the answer you think is correct. If you do not immediately know the correct answer, or you would like to review your answer at the end, write a question mark behind that question. This indicates that you flagged the answer for later review, so you do not waste time if you are stuck (very useful during the actual exam as well!).

Afterward, go to the answer section of this booklet. The answer key is provided, which allows you to determine your score. An explanation is provided in the last section of this booklet. Keep in mind that it is important to understand the logic behind the questions and answers, since that is one of the benefits of using this practice exam.

D1731101

About this document:

The practice exams currently available are incomplete, expensive, and treacherously easy. This practice exam provides you with more of a challenge than the alternatives. The brief explanations should help you understand the way questions can be phrased and how to choose the best answer.

After using this booklet as intended, combined with your regular study material, you should have improved your speed and accuracy, leaving you with sufficient time to go back to review the questions you flagged.

Good luck!

Kind regards,

Jasper Jacobs

EXAM QUESTIONS:

A state university has 2700 registered students. The students come from all over the US, but there are also several exchange students from other countries. The university tries hard to attract these international exchange students, for example by advertising on international student websites. The university provides both classroom courses and online courses, and takes pride in saving the environment by becoming increasingly paperless.

The campus includes several dormitories, sports facilities, cafeterias, and a medical office. All of these collect personal information, such as food allergies and medical conditions. All data are stored on the central server that connects all facilities, including the personal information.

During classes, the professors do not provide any paper handouts. All notes are shared digitally, through a digital study environment. Assignments are also handed in through the digital study environment, and exams are administered by simultaneously starting the exam in the classroom.

To make sure the innovative teaching method is possible, all actions are logged. This concerns both the actions of the students and the actions of the staff. Every click is registered, each and every time. The privacy notice – which has to be accepted before a student can commence studying at the university – mentions that actions are registered *as needed*.

The university recently appointed a privacy officer, who is in charge of creating privacy policies and providing advice for the university's data storage and sharing practices. However, the privacy officer is not part of a dedicated privacy department and is the only employee that is concerned with privacy.

1. Before the university declares a certain piece of information *directory information*, which of the following is most likely required?
A. parental opt-in for students younger than 18 years old
B. the students' opt-in
C. the opportunity for students to opt-out
D. written instructions from the Department of Education

2. Which of the following is most likely true regarding foreign exchange students?
A. the General Data Protection Regulation applies to part of the student body
B. foreign exchange students enjoy less protection of their personal information compared to US students
C. no protection of personal information is in place unless there is public funding involved
D. foreign privacy laws have more influence compared to US privacy laws

3. When would the Health Insurance Portability and Accountability Act most likely apply to the medical office's practices?
A. for foreign exchange students
B. whenever the school charges the student for medical services by credit card
C. when cash is required to pay for the medical treatment
D. in case there is no public funding for the school

4. Which of the following types of information can most likely be shared freely?
A. medical records
B. dietary preferences
C. directory information
D. Grade Point Average

5. In case an external party gains unauthorized access to the servers of the university, what would be the privacy officer's biggest concern?

A. whether the hacker breached the firewall
B. whether the hacker installed ransomware
C. whether the hacker installed a virus infecting the entire network of the school, through which personal information is shared
D. whether the hacker accessed personal information

A medical research company is involved in all sorts of research. All its clients are big corporations that, despite generating huge profits, claim that their mission is to help society increase its lifespan and quality of life. These organizations set the targets for further research, based on recent medical breakthroughs.

The medical research company employs a staff of 350 medical researchers and has conducted extremely impressive research. It is in contact with most hospitals in North America, and it shows interest in the cases that are relevant for its research. Patients that are either relevant for studying the side effects of medication or the effectiveness of the medication are offered free help in exchange for taking part in the company's research.

As part of the screening of its potential research subjects, a general and medical background check is performed. It is important for the researchers that the subject has no debts or violent crimes in his/her criminal record. Genetic characteristics are also of interest to the medical research company because certain combinations of genetics are more relevant due to the part of the population they form.

All of the medical research company's computers are connected to a local network only, and connection to the internet is made through separate dedicated computers that do not allow file transfers. If a hacker wants to gain access to the data, the hacker would have to physically be present on the premises to an extent. This way of working is required by the medical research company's clients, and a data management company is hired to make sure the medical research company stays compliant.

6. What would the contracted data management company most likely be called?
A. business associate
B. data processor
C. third party processor
D. data manager

7. In this scenario, which agency outside of the Federal Trade Commission and Federal Communications Commission is most likely to enforce privacy?
A. the Department of Health and Human Services
B. the Department of Motor Vehicles
C. the Office of Legislative Affairs
D. the Department of Education

8. When would the Health Insurance Portability and Accountability Act privacy rule least likely be relevant?
A. when no doctors are involved
B. when consent has been provided by the patient
C. when the patients are underaged and parental consent has been provided
D. when the data are de-identified

9. If under the Health Information Technology for Economic and Clinical Health Act, a breach notification is required, which of the following is most likely true?
A. the company has 30 days to notify individuals after discovering the breach
B. the company has 60 days to notify individuals after discovering the breach
C. the Data Protection Authority determines the course of action the company needs to take
D. it is up to the Federal Trade Commission to prove a breach has taken place

10. If the medical company decides to analyze the types of data it uses and performs a data inventory, which of the following is most likely true?
A. legal liability is significantly reduced
B. data can be re-classified to fall outside the scope of certain legislation
C. all legal obligations are complied with
D. potential risks can be discovered and targeted action can be taken

A small convenience store in a close-knit community where everyone looks after each other has recently been the victim of a violent robbery. The cashier was shot in the neck and barely survived. When the robber fled the scene, the locals quickly caught on the perpetrator and kept him subdued until the police showed up.

After finding out what happened, the owner of the convenience store helped the cashier that was shot, by paying all his medical expenses. The insurance covered this for the largest part, so this did not cost him much money. The cashier soon recovered and went back to work.

To show his gratitude and make life easier for the employees of the convenience store, the owner set up a system of employee loans. For an extremely low interest rate, employees can borrow money from the convenience store for paying off other debts so that the lower interest rate will benefit the employees in the long run.

At some point, one of the employees paid back a $70,000 loan in one cash transaction. The employee in question was unwilling to provide details on how he came into this amount of cash, and the owner felt uncomfortable and decided to inform the police.

The police thanked the owner for informing them, as it is indeed suspicious. However, at the moment it is not on their list of priorities and they will not pursue it as a standalone case. Perhaps in the future, if other events require it, they will look into the employee further.

11. If a break-in occurred at the convenience store, resulting in the loss of a hardcopy file containing personal information, what type of control was likely broken?
A. a physical control
B. an administrative control
C. a technical control
D. a security control

12. Which of the following is most likely true regarding the $70,000 loan repayment?
A. since the balance is $0 after the transaction, the store owner is not obligated to do anything
B. the transaction was made in cash, hence no reporting requirement exists
C. since the interest rate is low, the Internal Revenue Service does not need to be informed
D. since it was paid off in cash, at once, it needs to be reported to the Internal Revenue Service

13. Even though the convenience store owner does not use consumer reports to decide whether to issue a loan or not, which of the following could still be required?
A. report loans over $5,000
B. require loans to be paid back within a certain timeframe
C. the implementation of a Red Flag program
D. charge interest for amounts above $10,000

14. In case the convenience store owner did first request a consumer report before issuing a loan, which of the following would most likely be required when refusing a loan?
A. mentioning that they have 90 days to request a copy of the consumer report from the Consumer Reporting Agency
B. mentioning that it was not the Consumer Reporting Agency that took the decision
C. mentioning the contact details of the privacy officer of the convenience store
D. mentioning the contact details of the privacy officer of the Consumer Reporting Agency

15. In case the police want to investigate the customer who made the $70,000 cash transaction, and uses a wiretap, which of the following will most likely be required?
A. the Fourth Amendment prevents wiretaps in this case
B. a general warrant
C. probable cause
D. a private investigator

Gold4Cash is a US-based company that exchanges old cash for gold. Literally anyone with some money can enter the shop and exchange it for gold. No paperwork is required because only amounts of money below $1000 are exchanged for gold.

The concept becomes a great success. As a result, the company expands and opens new locations in Europe and Asia. There, it also is a great hit, and the company gets all kinds of free advertising on social media and regular TV.

As a consequence of branching out to Europe and Asia, the employee data of those countries need to be exchanged with payroll, which is located right next to the source of the gold, in Alaska. To facilitate this, the company is in the process of complying with the APEC Cross-Border Privacy Rules System and the conditions of the *standard contractual clauses*. The company considers this to be sufficient and tells its stores in Europe and Asia that no additional safeguards need to be in place. The European and Asian employees are aware of the international data transfers but assume it is fine because they were told about compliance with the APEC Cross-Border Privacy Rules System and the standard contractual clauses.

Despite the source of the gold being so close to Canada, the company has no desire to open a branch in Canada. Canadian citizens frequently cross the border to Alaska to exchange their money for gold, hence there is no need in the eyes of the CEO.

16. In India, where Gold4Cash has an affiliate, which of the following is most likely to be considered sensitive information?
A. social security number
B. iris scan on the employee ID
C. dietary preference
D. the employee's signature

17. Regarding the processing of personal information by Gold4Cash in case the CEO changes his mind and opens up a shop in Canada, which of the following is most likely the case?
A. if the standard contractual clauses (or model clauses) are signed, the transfers are free to take place
B. a data processing agreement needs to be in place
C. the Personal Information Protection and Electronic Documents Act applies
D. Canadian state laws are the greatest source of privacy

18. Which of the following Fair Information Practices is most likely violated?
A. Choice
B. Consent
C. Notice
D. Data subject access

19. Which of the following is required for their customers in the European Union?
A. a privacy notice during the collection of personal information
B. a sign at the entrance of the shop indicating personal data will be collected
C. a privacy notice before collecting personal information
D. obtaining consent before collecting personal information

20. Which of the following would be considered sensitive personal data in the European Union?
A. employee's bank account number
B. employee's background check results
C. employee's membership of a union
D. employee's appraisal file

A popular small craft brewery is considered to brew the finest IPA in the world. Its homegrown hop variety adds an intense yet palatable piney flavor to the beer. With the recent beer craze, the company has caught the attention of several large breweries. All of them make an offer to buy the small brewery to gain ownership of its exclusive hop variety.

The head brewer was heavily opposed to the idea of selling at first. However, after a period of moderate reflection, it became clear that there might be altruistic aspects to allowing the exploitation of the brewery's recipes and plants on a larger scale, despite losing control. To assist him in making his decision, he creates a website in every country, to solicit feedback on the decision, because he wants to test the waters in other continents.

As a free service, one of the large breweries that is interested in the small brewery offers its marketing and legal team to assist in the campaign. Shocked, the legal department urges the small brewery to implement an age check on the website, to make sure that only those of legal drinking age are able to enter the website where feedback is solicited. In addition, an internal meeting is organized to discuss what to do with the results that were obtained before the age check was implemented.

21. If the small brewery is targeting children to inquire about their parents' beer consumption, and follows a Children's Online Privacy Protection Act compliance code, which of the following is required?
A. co-regulation
B. approval of the Federal Trade Commission
C. approval of the Federal Communications Commission
D. approval of the Data Protection Authority

22. If the brewer is located in California, which of the following is most pressing for local visitors in case a third-party web beacon is used?
A. a data processing agreement with the web beacon user
B. a privacy notice
C. a secure HTTPS connection
D. inform visitors that third parties are collecting personal information

23. In case the brewer wants to supplement his web-based marketing campaign with a telephone campaign, which of the following does the brewery need to be able to consult the Do Not Call registry?
A. a robocall license
B. a signed statement declaring adherence to relevant legislation
C. a subscription account number
D. a Children's Online Privacy Protection Act compliance code

24. The brewer's marketing page contains a third-party web beacon. Which third party most likely provided the web beacon?
A. a social media website
B. the larger brewer wishing to buy the smaller brewer
C. the Federal Trade Commission
D. the Federal Communications Commission

25. When would the Controlling the Assault of Non-Solicited Pornography and Marketing Act most likely require the brewery to include a warning label in its commercial marketing e-mails?
A. if the alcohol percentage of the beer the e-mail pertains to exceeds 6.5% and the beer qualifies as strong liquor
B. if the logo used by the brewery for one of its beers contains a naked person
C. if it concerns a mass e-mail, not addressed to a specific person
D. if there is no prior business relationship with the addressees

A US government agency that deals with policies in North America is cracking down on laziness within the agency. From a recent survey, it became clear that the employees of the agency have a bad reputation, and are considered to be extremely lazy and unfriendly.

To combat the bad image, an advertisement campaign is started, acknowledging the reputation and promising to work hard to change the culture within the agency. Internally, a carrot and stick approach is used. Employees that achieve good results are rewarded with the possibility to attend interesting training and conferences, whereas employees that show incompetence or lethargy are suspended without pay.

The feedback from the survey showed that employees were often away from the desk where citizens were coming for assistance, either on smoke breaks or bathroom breaks. To verify any similar complaints in the future, CCTV cameras are placed outside the restroom and in the smoking area.

Sure enough, a complaint from an angry citizen arrives, and the director of the agency checks the footage of the CCTV cameras. The employee in question is not found to be either smoking or in the restroom for an extended period. However, the director does see two other employees of the opposite sex passionately enter the men's room at the moment he checks the live feed. Without giving it a second thought, he runs in and catches the two employees in the act.

26. If one or more of the employees initiate litigation, which tort is least likely to be used?
A. intrusion upon seclusion
B. unreasonable invasion of property
C. publicity given to private life
D. defamation

27. Before starting employment, a comprehensive overview of the privacy practices, including the use of CCTV, is provided to the employees. Which type of person is most likely not going to read the document?
A. the privacy unconcerned
B. the privacy pragmatists
C. the privacy liberalists
D. the privacy utilitarian

28. Which type of risk is least present in the workplace at this government agency?
A. reputational risk
B. investment risk
C. organizational risk
D. legal risk

29. In case the agency uses a contractor to maintain and operate the CCTV cameras, which of the following is most likely true?
A. the contractor is responsible for creating an inventory of laws the agency is required to comply with, and adapt their practices
B. the agency needs to assure that the contractor is compliant with the agency's privacy policy
C. the contractor is required to hire a privacy officer
D. the agency's privacy officer is required to approve the installing of CCTV cameras

30. When the CCTV cameras are filming inconsistently due to a malfunction, which of the following is most likely affected?
A. confidentiality
B. integrity
C. availability
D. distribution

Donald is a middle-aged US citizen that worked a mediocre job all his life and almost fully paid off his student debt. He has never missed a payment or gotten into financial trouble in any other way and decided not to spend more money than absolutely necessary until he has paid off his student debt in full.

One day, he finds his dream job. He truly feels the universe is rewarding him for his years of hard work. However, the company performs a background check after Donald is hired. The background check results in quite a bit of dirt and the company informs Donald that it has changed its mind.

Furiously Donald asks the company to explain further. The company explains that the background check shows Donald went bankrupt before and has made some terrible investments in the hotel sector. Donald informs them this is false, and that it must be a different Donald, but the company trusts the report it received from the Consumer Reporting Agency over Donald's word.

Donald's previous employer hears about what happened and offers to take Donald back on the condition that he undergoes a polygraph test to verify that nothing of concern to them has happened. Happy to return to work, Donald agrees. During the polygraph test the question regarding diseases in the family comes up, and the employer finds out Donald has an above-average risk to get early-onset Alzheimer's. He is not rehired, ends up on the street, and passes away shortly after.

31. Which of the following, besides the Federal Trade Commission and Federal Communications Commission, is most likely concerned with Donald's privacy in this scenario?
A. the Department of Education
B. the Department of Health Services
C. the Office of Legislative Affairs
D. the Equal Employment Opportunity Commission

32. If Donald wishes to litigate, when can he start?
A. if the background check was performed without a permissible purpose
B. if not performed for evaluating his candidacy
C. if he has not approved the performance of a background check
D. if the background check goes back to his high school years

33. If Donald's bankruptcy were indeed real, where could he possibly find a source of privacy protection?
A. the Bankruptcy Act
B. the Equal Employment Opportunity Commission
C. the Inmate Rehabilitation Act
D. the Fair and Accurate Credit Transactions Act

34. Before obtaining a consumer report from a Consumer Reporting Agency, what must the company have done according to Section 604(f) of the Fair Credit Reporting Act?
A. notified Donald that adverse action might be taken
B. disclosed to Donald that the company will obtain a consumer report
C. certified that the consumer report will be used for permissible purposes
D. informed Donald of his right to receive a free copy of his credit score annually

35. If, as a compromise, the company that rejected Donald offers to let him take a lie detector test to correct their information. Which of the following is most likely true?
A. the company is not allowed to use the results Donald offers of a lie detector test he administered at an independent agency
B. the company is only allowed to administer a psychological stress test
C. the company is only allowed to administer a polygraph test
D. the company is only allowed to administer a voice stress test

An application that can be installed on cell phones called *Cycle-Chat* allows those going for long bicycle rides to connect to those at home who would like to enjoy the view of the bicycle tour. In return, those enjoying the view at home are requested to cheer the cyclist on at the times when the cycling gets tough.

The cell phone is placed in a small contraption on the cyclist's bicycle. This contraption allows those connected with the phone of the cyclist to turn the camera of the phone to the view they wish to see. The idea is that it is a non-recorded session, and there is an incentive for users to return rather than re-watch a previously recorded bicycle ride.

Cycle-Chat turns out to be a great success. It has thousands of users, especially in mountain areas. One of its positive effects is that it allows the users at home to inform the emergency services in case the cyclist falls. This has encouraged a large number of lonely cyclists to become more active and wipe the dust off their old racing bicycles.

However, at the peak of its success, hackers gained access to the passwords of all users. These were stored without any hashing. In addition, it turned out that through a third-party patch on the application, users were able to store the entire exchange, unlike what was promulgated in Cycle-Chat's privacy statement.

36. What does it mean that Cycle-Chat stored passwords without hashing them?
A. only a 256-bit decryption device was needed to open the password file
B. the firewall could easily be bypassed to reach the passwords
C. the passwords were improperly compressed
D. the passwords were directly readable without any decoding

37. In case Cycle-Chat stores the video streams to later develop a biking video usable for home trainers, which of the following is likely true?
A. storing the video streams is a deceptive trade practice, as this is the opposite of what was communicated to the users
B. if the streams are de-identified before sending them to the contractor that develops the video collection for home trainers, there is no issue
C. the users are required to be informed afterward and should be presented with a choice on any future capturing of their video streams
D. given that the privacy notice is allowed to be changed at any moment, Cycle-Chat has the freedom to process personal information in any way it desires

38. Given the similarities to the SnapChat case, what will likely happen?
A. a consent decree will be issued, where Cycle-Chat admits guilt and promises improvement
B. there will be no consequences for Cycle-Chat, as it is a powerless victim of hacking
C. the security officer will be replaced as a consequence of Federal Trade Commission intervention
D. a consent order for not engaging in these business practices for 20 years will be entered into

39. If the breach were required to be communicated, at which point would this most likely have been the case?
A. at the most expeditious time and without unreasonable delay
B. as soon as possible
C. immediately after the final investigation is concluded
D. five business days after the breach was identified

40. If the hack occurred in 2003, in which state would the consequences for Cycle-Chat most likely be highest?
A. New York
B. California
C. Ohio
D. Florida

A company called *Medical4all* supplies homeopathic medication, which can be ordered directly on its website without any prescription. The homeopathic medication in its catalog consists of every piece of alternative medication imaginable, whether proven to work or not. In addition, it covers some conventional over-the-counter medicine that is at times covered by their customers' medical insurance.

Recently you have been hired by the company as a security and privacy officer. You are helping the company to both fend off attacks from those hacktivists aggressively opposing the spread of homeopathic medication because they claim it prevents people from seeking the medical care they need, as well as advising the company on how to deal with the large amount of sensitive data it handles.

At some point, you figure out that a few weeks before you started working for the company, there was an unauthorized access to a large amount of customer data. One consequence was that the purchase histories could be viewed. The logs reveal that within a short period, over 75% of the customer files have been accessed, and it cannot be excluded that a copy was made.

The CEO of the website is not worried. She even reveals that they sell a list of customers to a pharmaceutical marketing agency, which uses it to deliver targeted advertisements through social media.

41. Under which law will it most likely be required to report the breach?
A. the Health Information Technology for Economic and Clinical Health Act
B. the Health Insurance Portability and Accountability Act
C. the Children's Online Privacy Protection Act
D. the Health Care Data Breach Act

42. If the website also targets citizens in the European Union, what would the biggest objection against selling a list of customers to a marketing agency be?

A. the Data Protection Authority in Europe would be able to conduct an investigation

B. consent from part of the individuals on the list would be required

C. a data processing agreement would be required before selling the list

D. the company would liable for what third parties do with the list

43. Which of the following best describes the selling of a list of customers to a marketing agency?

A. an unfair trade practice

B. a data breach

C. a deceptive trade practice

D. a security incident

44. The website collects IP addresses. When is an IP address most likely to be considered personal information?

A. when it is dynamic

B. when the IP address is from a country in the European Union

C. when it is static

D. when the IP address is from the US

45. A customer file consists of the customer's name, purchase history, IP address, web activity, and shipping address. Which of the elements need to be removed to ensure the customer file is not personal information anymore?

A. customer name

B. customer name, IP address, shipping address

C. customer name, IP address, web activity, and shipping address

D. customer name, shipping address

A large international banking corporation based in the US, which offers services to both individuals and companies. The corporation has a large customer base. It has millions of clients globally and as a result processes millions of transactions on a daily basis.

Recently interest rates have dropped, and so has the banking corporation's profit. To compensate for this, the banking corporation started creating profiles of clients, based on the transactions that customers perform. For example, if several transactions in a sporting goods store show up, it is added to that person's profile that the person is interested in sports. If several transactions in a short period of time in a baby clothes shop show up, a label of *parent* is added to that person's profile.

Based on these transactions, targeted advertisement is shown to the clients. This occurs through the advertisement space on the banking corporation's website being sold based on the profiles of its users. If a person classified as being into sports logs in, within a millisecond, a signal is sent to the advertisement provider, and a sports-related advertisement is displayed.

The targeted advertisement proves to be quite lucrative, and the banking corporation decides to take it to the next level. Lists of phone numbers, addresses, and e-mail addresses are sold to whoever is interested, including the profile attached to each individual.

46. If, based on the profiles created by the bank, hackers target an individual and send e-mails tailored to that person, with malicious software to gain entry to that individual's bank account, what would this be called?
A. spam
B. social engineering
C. spear phishing
D. unauthorized access

47. If, in addition to digital advertising, the bank starts calling customers, which of the following will least likely reduce the bank's liability in case something goes wrong?
A. a written procedure about not calling unwanted
B. trained personnel
C. a data inventory
D. a Do Not Call list specifically for the bank

48. The bank sells the list to a company but misspelled the addressee's e-mail address. What type of data breach is this most likely?
A. unintended disclosure
B. physical loss
C. insider
D. hacking or malware

49. In this scenario, the practices most likely violate which of the following rights from the Consumer Privacy Bill of Rights?
A. access and accuracy
B. security
C. purpose limitation
D. respect for context

50. From a General Data Protection Regulation perspective, what role does the bank most likely have at the moment it is selling lists of contact data?
A. a processor
B. a business associate
C. a third party
D. a controller

Organizations often use software to create an overview of their data processing, types of data they collect, classifications, data breaches, and other privacy or security-related information. Software packages for this purpose are widely available, and given the large number of providers of such software packages, they are relatively cheap.

You work for a company that sells domain names. There is really not much to it, except recording where a visitor is supposed to be guided to when a certain domain name is entered into a web browser. The list of customers is not stored on a server connected to the internet, only on a local server to which the building has access.

Given the recent privacy and security trend, and the developments in legislation, your company has purchased an online software package called *Privacy Safe*. An inventory of all processes is created using the software, as well as a label of the category of data, after which the software indicates which laws are applicable and what the possible restrictions are. In addition, in case of a data breach, this can be recorded using the software, and a report with action points will be generated.

Then, ironically, the company that sells Privacy Safe was the victim of a cyber-attack. All data were accessed, including the databases of the company's customers. This means the data you entered in the software for your organization were also accessed.

51. In which case is a data inventory as described in this scenario likely mandatory?
A. if an institution is covered by the Family Educational Rights and Privacy Act
B. in case the organization transfers personal information to Canadian government institutions
C. if the Chief Information Security Officer has deemed the inventory mandatory
D. if an institution is covered by the Gramm-Leach-Bliley Act

52. The Privacy Safe software did not encrypt the data properly. Which case is this similar to?
A. Lifelock Inc.
B. Vulcan
C. Geocities Inc.
D. Nomi

53. If the Privacy Safe software contains an HTML part containing a pixel that registers the IP address that loads each time the software is started, what would that be called?
A. a log pixel
B. a monitoring pixel
C. a web beacon
D. user tracking file

54. Which of the following will least likely be considered processing of personal information?
A. keeping a file containing categories of personal information
B. printing a list of e-mail addresses
C. logging the access of wireless devices on the network
D. requiring the scan of a badge where access rights are granted to employees' badge number

55. If the company wants to share its cyber threat indicators, what is required first?
A. the removal of identifiers
B. permission from those involved
C. Federal Trade Commission approval
D. Federal Communications Commission approval

The Federal Bureau of Investigation is investigating a person suspected of hatching terrorist plans. An anonymous tip was sent to the Federal Bureau of Investigation by a concerned citizen who attends the same religious gatherings as the suspect. The anonymous tip contains the information that the suspect takes the religious texts that are provided to him literally, and is unable to place them in a modern-day context. The suspect recently acquired several weapons, legally.

According to the Federal Bureau of Investigation's records, the suspect indeed purchased two weapons recently, which can cause a lot of damage if used inappropriately. This in itself is not unusual, but combined with the tip from the anonymous person they consider there to be sufficient reason to place a wiretap and intercept the suspect's e-mail exchange.

You are an employee of the internet provider of the suspect and have been requested by the Federal Bureau of Investigation to assist in the interception of his e-mails. Since the e-mail uses the encryption your company has implemented, the Federal Bureau of Investigation needs your help to decipher the intercepted data.

At first you are reluctant, because the Federal Bureau of Investigation does not share any information as to why the suspect is under investigation. In addition, you find out that the suspect was a citizen of the EU prior to becoming a US citizen, and there could be some applicable restrictions following from the General Data Protection Regulation.

56. When shipping the discovered evidence on a physical medium, which of the following would you consider most important from a legal point of view?
A. shipping on Solid State Drives
B. shipping in a way that preserves an audit trail
C. shipping with adequately protected backups
D. shipping files with 256-bit encryption

57. If the data of the suspect are stored largely in Europe, which of the following might provide restrictions regarding the access to the data?
A. the Personal Information Protection and Electronic Documents Act
B. the General Data Protection Regulation
C. the Protection of Personal Information Act
D. the CLOUD Act

58. If in the privacy notice, your company has promised its clients not to share their personal information with third parties, including law enforcement, what could happen if you do provide access to the Federal Bureau of Investigation?
A. section 5 of the Federal Trade Commission Act could be enforced
B. the evidence gathered is inadmissible in court
C. an automatic fine is triggered
D. the client has the authority to call the gathering of evidence to a halt

59. Under the computer trespasser exception, if applicable, which of the following statement is most appropriate?
A. you are obliged to cooperate
B. you are not allowed to cooperate without a warrant
C. you are not allowed to provide instruction but are allowed to provide access
D. you are free to cooperate, as well as free to refuse cooperation

60. If the Federal Bureau of Investigation wants to intercept the e-mail of the suspect, what is generally required?
A. a subpoena
B. a warrant
C. a court order or other lawful basis
D. encryption

A gigantic marketing campaign has been launched for a new electric toothbrush. People are encouraged to take part in a lottery, for which they have to fill out a form with a few questions. Those with the correct answers are entered into the lottery, with a vacation to Paris for the winner and a few electric toothbrushes to be given away to a few less lucky contestants.

When entering the lottery, a notice is provided that states that your personal information will be used to make this lottery possible. The example regarding your address is mentioned, as in that the company needs your address to ship your prize in case you win. This makes it seem as if the marketing campaign stops after the lottery.

However, long after the lottery ended, the list with personal information on all contestants is still kept by the company. The company intends to use it in case there are other marketing campaigns, although this was not indicated in the notice provided to people when signing up for the lottery.

The toothbrush company is doing well, after which the CEO decides to sell it. Its technology and customer service department are bought by a competitor. This competitor is mostly interested in the technology that was embedded in the toothbrush because it has the ability to change programming based on the user's brushing habits.

61. The toothbrush connects to open WIFI connections if it detects them, and transmits data about the frequency of its use to the manufacturer. What can be said about the data transmitted to the manufacturer?
A. the amount of use of a toothbrush is personal information
B. no permission is required from the user
C. this could be considered sensitive personal data in Europe, depending on the other data a manufacturer can link to that specific device
D. a notice informing the user of the connection to WIFI is not required, as it does not transmit anything about the user, only about the device

62. Which of the following is in line with the purposes identified in the notice?
A. storing the personal information
B. selling the personal information
C. re-using the personal information
D. using the personal information for marketing purposes

63. If the toothbrush connects to WIFI, what is this type of phenomenon commonly referred to?
A. device enabled Personal Information sharing
B. human-device exposure
C. Virtual Reality
D. the Internet of Things

64. If the toothbrush company enters into a consent decree with the Federal Trade Commission, which of the following is most likely true?
A. the Federal Trade Commission has one-sidedly forced the company to pay a fine
B. a judge ordered the illegal activity to come to a halt, and for the company to pay a fine in case it violates the consent decree
C. the company committed unfair and deceptive practices
D. it agrees to stop the alleged wrong activity without admitting wrongdoing

65. If the toothbrush company has entered into a consent decree regarding its privacy practices, and seemingly violates that consent decree, what is most likely to happen?
A. a Federal Trade Commission investigation
B. enforcement in the Federal District court
C. civil penalties
D. injunctions

After going through a tough period, having taken many wrong turns, your life is slowly starting to get back on track. You have battled with drug addiction for years, and after treatment in a well-known clinic, you have completely kicked the habit.

You get back to your old life, and your family, friends, and colleagues understand your situation and give you all the support you need. In addition, you attend a support group every two weeks, where you discuss your experiences with those who share the same fate to some extent.

All is going well, and you stay clean. Your doctor prescribes you tablets that help you with keeping the urges away, which are fully covered by your health insurance. Obviously, you accept all the help you can get, and diligently use the medication as prescribed.

One day, your spouse sits you down and looks at you angrily. It turns out a pharmaceutical company has phoned, asking your oldest child how the withdrawal symptoms are and whether they can send you their newest medication. Your child now knows you had a drug problem.

66. When will the clinic least likely be subject to the Health Insurance Portability and Accountability Act for your treatment?
A. if you pay in cash out of your own pocket
B. if one of the privacy rule exemptions applies
C. if the program receives federal funding
D. if the clinic is run by volunteers

67. The clinic wants to sell the information subject to the Drug Abuse, Prevention, Treatment and Rehabilitation Act. What would most likely allow this?
A. a legitimate interest
B. the patient's written consent
C. a court order
D. a subpoena

68. Which of the following fits the definition of patient-identifying information best, in the context of the clinic?
A. any information that can directly or indirectly identify a person diagnosed with substance abuse
B. any information related to a natural person
C. any information regarding the type of drug a person abused
D. the status of the patient in his or her rehabilitation process

69. If the pharmaceutical company has received your name on a list which it bought from the clinic, which case would this be similar to?
A. Eli Lilly & Co
B. TRENDnet Inc.
C. Geocities Inc.
D. DesignerWare LLC

70. If the treatment clinic received federal funding for the program you took part in, which of the following can least likely be done with your Personal Information?
A. use the information in a way that can lead to criminal charges against the patient
B. use the information in a way that can lead to criminal charges
C. use your written information
D. use your verbally provided information

One afternoon you arrive home from work early and hear the door closing in the back of the house. You cautiously explore the house and find your wife on the couch in lingerie. When you ask her who just left and why she is wearing lingerie, she says she just entered the house and was waiting in the backyard to see you arrive and surprise you.

After foolishly believing your wife and having a wonderful afternoon, doubt starts to kick in. You cannot grasp why she would wait for you in the backyard rather than just observe through the window. She must be unfaithful to you. You decide to hire a private investigator to find out more.

The private investigator comes back with the news that your wife is indeed cheating on you. In fact, she even seduced the private investigator, which he shows you on the footage of the hidden camera he placed in his van where your wife followed him to.

Immediately you want to file for divorce. However, you want to approach things with caution, to make sure your wife gets the least possible in the divorce. You are not sure to which extent the evidence you have gathered is legal and allowed to be used.

71. If your wife's lawyer sends you a request to hand over the records the private investigator created of her, which form would that request most likely be in?
A. a subpoena
B. a warrant
C. a national security letter
D. a compliance note

72. When your wife requests the fact that it was her birthday the day she cheated on you with the private investigator be left out of the information provided during e-discovery, what is this most likely called?
A. redaction
B. restriction
C. legal editing
D. relevance testing

73. In case the court is not covered by the Federal Rules of Civil Procedure, and your wife wishes the medical information supporting her case supplied by her health insurance not to be made public, which of the following can most likely provide help?
A. a qualified protective order
B. the Health Information Technology for Economic and Clinical Health Act disclosure restriction
C. an extended Federal Rules of Civil Procedure application
D. the Fourth Amendment

74. If the court orders the information revealed about the behavior of your wife not to be disclosed outside the courtroom, what would this most likely be referred to?
A. information restriction
B. e-discovery limitation
C. protective order
D. the Fourth Amendment right to prevent unreasonable disclosure

75. If your wife is served a subpoena, but does not obey, what is most likely going to happen?
A. forfeiture of the court case
B. a fine or prison
C. she will be excluded from the e-discovery process
D. a new date for the court case will have to be established

A small bakery started a surprise bread service tit calls *bread of the world*, where the bakery bakes different types of bread and delivers them to its customers. Of course, the point of the bread service is to taste different kinds of bread, so the bakery decided that its customers buy a subscription after which the bread is delivered.

In order not to cause any health issues, customers are requested to fill out a form indicating any food-related allergies they have. This way, with the variety of bread styles, a customer will not receive the weekly bread if it contains any of the dangerous allergens.

A database with all customers, their allergies, and their credit card numbers is stored on the local computer in the bakery. The computer is connected to the internet since a large part of the bakery's customers order through the bakery's website.

One day, the owner turns on the computer and sees a message displayed on the screen, stating that a certain amount of cryptocurrency needs to be paid to unlock the computer. It turns out, a malicious file was opened and the computer got infected with malware. The owner picks up his computer and smashes it, hoping to solve the problem this way.

76. If the bakery were located in the European Union, what could provide an issue?
A. consent would be required for all processing of personal data
B. the Health Insurance Portability and Accountability Act applies to allergy information
C. the allergy information could be considered sensitive personal data
D. the Data Protection Authority needs to be informed of the processing

77. Which of the following would result in the most secure storage of the sensitive files the bakery processes, such as allergy information and financial information?
A. using a firewall
B. compressing the files to make them more difficult for hackers to find
C. scanning for viruses regularly
D. using encryption and storing the data offline

78. Which of the following would least likely be considered a transactional or relationship message?
A. an e-mail to confirm an order
B. an e-mail to inform about a change in the delivery schedule
C. an e-mail to inform the customer that it can return the bread of last week and receive a refund
D. an e-mail to potential customers that have been suggested by existing customers

79. One day the bakery chats with a customer, explaining it is preparing the bread baskets for the diabetic customers. On one of the baskets, the customer sees the name of one of the applicants for the job she is conducting interviews for next week. What will most likely prevent her from doing anything with the information?
A. the Genetic Information and Nondiscrimination Act
B. the Health Insurance Portability and Accountability Act
C. the Health Information Technology for Economic and Clinical Health Act
D. the state data breach legislation

80. In case the bakery provides a notice of what the bakery will do with your data and the services it delivers, after which you decide to share your personal information, what needs to be present for the privacy notice to be considered a contract?
A. both parties agreeing to the terms
B. terms for changing the practices
C. an offer, acceptance, and consideration
D. a third reviewing party

A hotel chain has recently been involved in a scandal. One staff member was upset over the low salary and the hotel's policy of collecting all tips and distributing them evenly over the staff. To get revenge, she placed cameras in the rooms of the hotel guests. The disgruntled employee also had access to the guest registry.

Access to the live streams was sold on the dark web. The live streams of high-profile hotel guests resulted in the highest price. It took several years for the practice to be discovered by law enforcement, and happened after a guest was sent images of himself with his mistress.

To add to the scandal, someone who considered himself a cyber vigilante made an anonymous phone call to the police anytime a crime showed up on the live stream. This included anything without consent.

Finally, when a politician was discovered with an underaged child, someone watching the live stream intervened and broke into the hotel room to save the child. The whole live stream was recorded and sent to the police as evidence. This resulted in the hidden camera practice being uncovered.

81. What would have most significantly lowered the chances of this incident occurring?
A. frequent audits on the WIFI network
B. forbidding Virtual Private Network connection over the WIFI servers
C. providing the personnel with security training
D. appointing a Chief Information Security Officer

82. If the video stream cannot be traced back to the hotel, which of the following is most untrue?
A. there is a significant invasion of privacy
B. it does not matter whether the location is known, the chance of the person on the video being identified results in it containing personal information
C. the level of responsibility of the hotel depends, to an extent, on which controls it has in place to prevent these types of incidents
D. the video stream no longer contains personal information

83. In case the perpetrator installed wireless devices that connected with a cell phone tower to transmit the video stream, which of the following is the most likely to reveal the source of the perpetrator?
A. the telecom company
B. the hotel's human resources department
C. the perpetrator
D. the users of the video stream

84. The security officer has detected a stream of data that could not be read. What is most likely the case?
A. the stream was sent over a Virtual Private Network connection
B. the compression was unable to keep up
C. unsupported formats were used
D. the codec of the video steam was uniquely hashed

85. To which of the following cases is this case similar?
A. Lifelock Inc.
B. TRENDnet
C. Designerware LLC
D. Vulcan

A small company has hired you to grow its sales team. You sell car insurance. It is what you have done your entire professional life, and it is what you are good at. Part of your tasks is to make cold calls and convince people to take out insurance or switch to the company's insurance policy.

Every morning you are provided with a list of names and phone numbers. The goal is to call all these numbers that day. Your phone log will be reviewed by the manager at the end of the week, and if the log does not correspond to the numbers on the list you have been provided with, there is a clarification meeting in which a justification needs to be provided.

You also receive a list of e-mails. This list has been obtained from a data broker, who tricked people into providing their personal details in order to win a non-existing prize. It is a large list, but all persons on the list have been categorized by the data broker as owning one or more vehicles.

Before starting work, your colleagues tell you that the e-mails you send are read by the manager. Not only your work e-mail but also the personal messages sent over the company's network. You are not quite sure how this is done, but it may have something to do with the staff application you were obliged to install on your phone before being allowed to commence work.

86. If the data broker gathered his data from public sources, which of the following APEC principles is least relevant?
A. Security safeguards
B. Accountability
C. Choice
D. Preventing harm

87. If the data broker performed an internet sweep through several sources of public data, which of the following APEC principles is most likely not respected?
A. Accountability
B. Collection limitation
C. Security safeguards
D. Access and correction

88. The company's sales practices are most likely impacted by which of the following?
A. strict state law
B. the Fourth amendment
C. the Controlling the Assault of Non-Solicited Pornography and Marketing Act
D. the Children's Online Privacy Protection Act

89. If the company allows employees to use their own laptops and smartphones to perform their work, which of the following could likely provide the most privacy protection?
A. state law
B. a Bring Your Own Device Policy signed by both parties
C. an employment manual
D. national law

90. If the company ignores the Do Not Call registry when contacting someone, what would you hope as a privacy officer to be the case?
A. the calls take place outside of the restricted hours
B. the calls take place within business hours
C. only authorized robocalls take place
D. an existing relationship within the last 18 months

CORRECT ANSWERS:

1C	31D	61C
2A	32A	62A
3D	33A	63D
4C	34C	64D
5D	35A	65A
6A	36D	66A
7A	37A	67B
8D	38D	68A
9B	39A	69C
10D	40B	70A
11A	41A	71A
12D	42B	72A
13C	43C	73A
14B	44C	74C
15C	45C	75B
16B	46C	76C
17C	47C	77D
18C	48A	78D
19C	49D	79A
20C	50D	80C
21B	51D	81C
22D	52A	82D
23C	53C	83A
24A	54A	84A
25B	55A	85C
26B	56B	86C
27A	57B	87B
28B	58A	88C
29B	59D	89B
30B	60C	90D

QUESTIONS WITH BRIEF EXPLANATIONS:

A state university has 2700 registered students. The students come from all over the US, but there are also several exchange students from other countries. The university tries hard to attract these international exchange students, for example by advertising on international student websites. The university provides both classroom courses and online courses, and takes pride in saving the environment by becoming increasingly paperless.

The campus includes several dormitories, sports facilities, cafeterias, and a medical office. All of these collect personal information, such as food allergies and medical conditions. All data are stored on the central server that connects all facilities, including the personal information.

During classes, the professors do not provide any paper handouts. All notes are shared digitally, through a digital study environment. Assignments are also handed in through the digital study environment, and exams are administered by simultaneously starting the exam in the classroom.

To make sure the innovative teaching method is possible, all actions are logged. This concerns both the actions of the students and the actions of the staff. Every click is registered, each and every time. The privacy notice – which has to be accepted before a student can commence studying at the university – mentions that actions are registered *as needed*.

The university recently appointed a privacy officer, who is in charge of creating privacy policies and providing advice for the university's data storage and sharing practices. However, the privacy officer is not part of a dedicated privacy department and is the only employee that is concerned with privacy.

1. Before the university declares a certain piece of information *directory information*, which of the following is most likely required?
A. parental opt-in for students younger than 18 years old
B. the students' opt-in
C. the opportunity for students to opt-out (correct)
D. written instructions from the Department of Education
Explanation:
Before something can be declared directory information, students need to be given the opportunity to opt out or block the information. Option C is the correct answer.

2. Which of the following is most likely true regarding foreign exchange students?
A. the General Data Protection Regulation applies to part of the student body (correct)
B. foreign exchange students enjoy less protection of their personal information compared to US students
C. no protection of personal information is in place unless there is public funding involved
D. foreign privacy laws have more influence compared to US privacy laws
Explanation:
Given that the university was actively targeting foreign students by advertising on international websites, including in the European Union, the General Data Protection Regulation is applicable for the processing of the personal information (personal data) of the students from the European Union. A is the correct answer.
Important to remember perhaps, is that not all European countries are part of the European Union, most notably the United Kingdom (after BREXIT).

3. When would the Health Insurance Portability and Accountability Act most likely apply to the medical office's practices?
A. for foreign exchange students
B. whenever the school charges the student for medical services by credit card
C. when cash is required to pay for the medical treatment
D. in case there is no public funding for the school (correct)
Explanation:
If the university receives no public funding, the Family Educational Rights and Privacy Act does not apply, making it more likely that the Health Insurance Portability and Accountability Act applies in the medical office. D is the correct answer.

4. Which of the following types of information can most likely be shared freely?
A. medical records
B. dietary preferences
C. directory information (correct)
D. Grade Point Average
Explanation:
Under the Family Education Rights and Privacy Act, directory information is allowed to be disclosed without student permission, hence C is the correct answer. The other options are not likely directory information.

5. In case an external party gains unauthorized access to the servers of the university, what would be the privacy officer's biggest concern?
A. whether the hacker breached the firewall
B. whether the hacker installed ransomware
C. whether the hacker installed a virus infecting the entire network of the school, through which personal information is shared
D. whether the hacker accessed personal information (correct)
Explanation:
When personal information has actually been accessed this brings along the highest likelihood of privacy being compromised (of the available options). D is the correct answer. In the other options, it is not necessarily the case that personal information has been accessed or processed in any way.

A medical research company is involved in all sorts of research. All its clients are big corporations that, despite generating huge profits, claim that their mission is to help society increase its lifespan and quality of life. These organizations set the targets for further research, based on recent medical breakthroughs.

The medical research company employs a staff of 350 medical researchers and has conducted extremely impressive research. It is in contact with most hospitals in North America, and it shows interest in the cases that are relevant for its research. Patients that are either relevant for studying the side effects of medication or the effectiveness of the medication are offered free help in exchange for taking part in the company's research.

As part of the screening of its potential research subjects, a general and medical background check is performed. It is important for the researchers that the subject has no debts or violent crimes in his/her criminal record. Genetic characteristics are also of interest to the medical research company because certain combinations of genetics are more relevant due to the part of the population they form.

All of the medical research company's computers are connected to a local network only, and connection to the internet is made through separate dedicated computers that do not allow file transfers. If a hacker wants to gain access to the data, the hacker would have to physically be present on the premises to an extent. This way of working is required by the medical research company's clients, and a data management company is hired to make sure the medical research company stays compliant.

6. What would the contracted data management company most likely be called?

A. business associate (correct)

B. data processor

C. third party processor

D. data manager

Explanation:

Third parties that process Personal Health Information for another party are called business associates in this scenario. A is the correct answer. B would be correct under the General Data Protection Regulation, and the other two answers are nonsense.

7. In this scenario, which agency outside of the Federal Trade Commission and Federal Communications Commission is most likely to enforce privacy?

A. the Department of Health and Human Services (correct)

B. the Department of Motor Vehicles

C. the Office of Legislative Affairs

D. the Department of Education

Explanation:

The Department of Health and Human Services is the least farfetched of the available options. A is the correct answer, which could have also been easily guessed. During the exam questions like this can be flagged for later review if you do not immediately know the answer.

8. When would the Health Insurance Portability and Accountability Act privacy rule least likely be relevant?

A. when no doctors are involved

B. when consent has been provided by the patient

C. when the patients are underaged and parental consent has been provided

D. when the data are de-identified (correct)

Explanation:

When the data are correctly de-identified, there is no way to trace (part of) them back to an individual, resulting in there not being much need for protecting privacy. D is the correct answer. Be sure that when there is a question about dc-identification or rendering data anonymous, that you ask yourself whether the right data elements have been removed.

9. If under the Health Information Technology for Economic and Clinical Health Act, a breach notification is required, which of the following is most likely true?

A. the company has 30 days to notify individuals after discovering the breach

B. the company has 60 days to notify individuals after discovering the breach (correct)

C. the Data Protection Authority determines the course of action the company needs to take

D. it is up to the Federal Trade Commission to prove a breach has taken place

Explanation:

The number of days to remember is 60 days, and after discovery (not investigation). B is the correct answer. When encountering a question regarding data breach notification that does not mention specific numbers, make sure to pick the most reasonable-sounding answer (such as at the earliest possible time or after establishing that personal information has been accessed).

10. If the medical company decides to analyze the types of data it uses and performs a data inventory, which of the following is most likely true?

A. legal liability is significantly reduced

B. data can be re-classified to fall outside the scope of certain legislation

C. all legal obligations are complied with

D. potential risks can be discovered and targeted action can be taken (correct)

Explanation:

A data inventory itself results in nothing more than an overview of which types of data you collect. This can be expanded by all sorts of additional information, such as identifying applicable laws, mapping the flows, etc. This could potentially identify risks, hence D is the correct answer. Option C would be correct if there is a law that requires insight into the personal information being processed (such as the General Data Protection Regulation), but that is not the case for this question.

A small convenience store in a close-knit community where everyone looks after each other has recently been the victim of a violent robbery. The cashier was shot in the neck and barely survived. When the robber fled the scene, the locals quickly caught on the perpetrator and kept him subdued until the police showed up.

After finding out what happened, the owner of the convenience store helped the cashier that was shot, by paying all his medical expenses. The insurance covered this for the largest part, so this did not cost him much money. The cashier soon recovered and went back to work.

To show his gratitude and make life easier for the employees of the convenience store, the owner set up a system of employee loans. For an extremely low interest rate, employees can borrow money from the convenience store for paying off other debts so that the lower interest rate will benefit the employees in the long run.

At some point, one of the employees paid back a $70,000 loan in one cash transaction. The employee in question was unwilling to provide details on how he came into this amount of cash, and the owner felt uncomfortable and decided to inform the police.

The police thanked the owner for informing them, as it is indeed suspicious. However, at the moment it is not on their list of priorities and they will not pursue it as a standalone case. Perhaps in the future, if other events require it, they will look into the employee further.

11. If a break-in occurred at the convenience store, resulting in the loss of a hardcopy file containing personal information, what type of control was likely broken?

A. a physical control (correct)

B. an administrative control

C. a technical control

D. a security control

Explanation:

Physically breaking in somewhere requires breaking physical controls. Technical and security controls could also be broken, but not necessarily, for example, if there is no security system in place. Therefore, option A is the most correct answer.

12. Which of the following is most likely true regarding the $70,000 loan repayment?

A. since the balance is $0 after the transaction, the store owner is not obligated to do anything

B. the transaction was made in cash, hence no reporting requirement exists

C. since the interest rate is low, the Internal Revenue Service does not need to be informed

D. since it was paid off in cash, at once, it needs to be reported to the Internal Revenue Service (correct)

Explanation:

Amounts above $10,000 need to be reported to the Internal Revenue Service. Option D is correct.

13. Even though the convenience store owner does not use consumer reports to decide whether to issue a loan or not, which of the following could still be required?

A. report loans over $5,000

B. require loans to be paid back within a certain timeframe

C. the implementation of a Red Flag program (correct)

D. charge interest for amounts above $10,000

Explanation:

A Red Flag program is required for all creditors. Since the convenience store provides loans, it could be the case that it is seen as a creditor and is required to implement a Red Flag program. Option C is the correct answer.

14. In case the convenience store owner did first request a consumer report before issuing a loan, which of the following would most likely be required when refusing a loan?
A. mentioning that they have 90 days to request a copy of the consumer report from the Consumer Reporting Agency
B. mentioning that it was not the Consumer Reporting Agency that took the decision (correct)
C. mentioning the contact details of the privacy officer of the convenience store
D. mentioning the contact details of the privacy officer of the Consumer Reporting Agency
Explanation:
It needs to be mentioned that the Consumer Reporting Agency did not take the decision. Option B is correct, the other options are incorrect. Option A would be correct if it mentioned 60 days instead of 90 days.

15. In case the police want to investigate the customer who made the $70,000 cash transaction, and uses a wiretap, which of the following will most likely be required?
A. the Fourth Amendment prevents wiretaps in this case
B. a general warrant
C. probable cause (correct)
D. a private investigator
Explanation:
For a wiretap probably cause is required. Option C is correct.

Gold4Cash is a US-based company that exchanges old cash for gold. Literally anyone with some money can enter the shop and exchange it for gold. No paperwork is required because only amounts of money below $1000 are exchanged for gold.

The concept becomes a great success. As a result, the company expands and opens new locations in Europe and Asia. There, it also is a great hit, and the company gets all kinds of free advertising on social media and regular TV.

As a consequence of branching out to Europe and Asia, the employee data of those countries need to be exchanged with payroll, which is located right next to the source of the gold, in Alaska. To facilitate this, the company is in the process of complying with the APEC Cross-Border Privacy Rules System and the conditions of the *standard contractual clauses*. The company considers this to be sufficient and tells its stores in Europe and Asia that no additional safeguards need to be in place. The European and Asian employees are aware of the international data transfers but assume it is fine because they were told about compliance with the APEC Cross-Border Privacy Rules System and the standard contractual clauses.

Despite the source of the gold being so close to Canada, the company has no desire to open a branch in Canada. Canadian citizens frequently cross the border to Alaska to exchange their money for gold, hence there is no need in the eyes of the CEO.

16. In India, where Gold4Cash has an affiliate, which of the following is most likely to be considered sensitive information?
A. social security number
B. iris scan on the employee ID (correct)
C. dietary preference
D. the employee's signature
Explanation:
In India, biometric information is considered sensitive information. Option B is correct. You will likely encounter a few questions on the exam like this, that may not have been covered in your study materials. Do not worry about it, as they could be non-scored questions. Just pick an answer that sounds reasonable and flag the question to come back to later in case you have time at the end of the exam.

17. Regarding the processing of personal information by Gold4Cash in case the CEO changes his mind and opens up a shop in Canada, which of the following is most likely the case?
A. if the standard contractual clauses (or model clauses) are signed, the transfers are free to take place
B. a data processing agreement needs to be in place
C. the Personal Information Protection and Electronic Documents Act applies (correct)
D. Canadian state laws are the greatest source of privacy
Explanation:
The Personal Information and Electronic Document Act is the Canadian law of which you will want to remember the name. Option C is correct. The gist of the law is that permission is required for every processing of personal information, unless one of the exceptions applies. The government in Canada falls under different laws.

18. Which of the following Fair Information Practices is most likely violated?
A. Choice
B. Consent
C. Notice (correct)
D. Data subject access
Explanation:
The information provided to the employees was incorrect and therefore answer C is more likely than the others. Whether the others are violated is (intentionally) not clear from the text.

19. Which of the following is required for their customers in the European Union?
A. a privacy notice during the collection of personal information
B. a sign at the entrance of the shop indicating personal data will be collected
C. a privacy notice before collecting personal information (correct)
D. obtaining consent before collecting personal information
Explanation:
Option C is correct. In the European Union (not all of Europe) every person needs to be informed about the details of the processing of their personal information (personal data).

20. Which of the following would be considered sensitive personal data in the European Union?
A. employee's bank account number
B. employee's background check results
C. employee's membership of a union (correct)
D. employee's appraisal file
Explanation:
Membership of a union is considered sensitive personal data. For more information see Article 9 of the General Data Protection Regulation. Option C is the correct answer.

A popular small craft brewery is considered to brew the finest IPA in the world. Its homegrown hop variety adds an intense yet palatable piney flavor to the beer. With the recent beer craze, the company has caught the attention of several large breweries. All of them make an offer to buy the small brewery to gain ownership of its exclusive hop variety.

The head brewer was heavily opposed to the idea of selling at first. However, after a period of moderate reflection, it became clear that there might be altruistic aspects to allowing the exploitation of the brewery's recipes and plants on a larger scale, despite losing control. To assist him in making his decision, he creates a website in every country, to solicit feedback on the decision, because he wants to test the waters in other continents.

As a free service, one of the large breweries that is interested in the small brewery offers its marketing and legal team to assist in the campaign. Shocked, the legal department urges the small brewery to implement an age check on the website, to make sure that only those of legal drinking age are able to enter the website where feedback is solicited. In addition, an internal meeting is organized to discuss what to do with the results that were obtained before the age check was implemented.

21. If the small brewery is targeting children to inquire about their parents' beer consumption, and follows a Children's Online Privacy Protection Act compliance code, which of the following is required?
A. co-regulation
B. approval of the Federal Trade Commission (correct)
C. approval of the Federal Communications Commission
D. approval of the Data Protection Authority
Explanation:
Children's Online Privacy Protection codes require approval from the Federal Trade Commission. Option B is the correct answer.

22. If the brewer is located in California, which of the following is most pressing for local visitors in case a third-party web beacon is used?
A. a data processing agreement with the web beacon user
B. a privacy notice
C. a secure HTTPS connection
D. inform visitors that third parties are collecting personal information (correct)
Explanation:
A third-party web beacon is usually a transparent pixel on a website that is loaded from the server of a third party, thereby allowing the third party to see which IP address (or other data) has loaded the pixel placed on a certain website, at what time, and how often. If the third party is a social media website, it can compare the IP address that loaded the pixel at a certain time with its users at that time. If there is a match with a certain user of the social media website, the social media website knows that this user also visited the website of the brewer. Option D is most correct, as this is potentially revealing quite some information to third parties.

23. In case the brewer wants to supplement his web-based marketing campaign with a telephone campaign, which of the following does the brewery need to be able to consult the Do Not Call registry?
A. a robocall license
B. a signed statement declaring adherence to relevant legislation
C. a subscription account number (correct)
D. a Children's Online Privacy Protection Act compliance code
Explanation:
A subscription account number is required to be able to consult the Do Not Call registry. Option C is correct.

24. The brewer's marketing page contains a third-party web beacon. Which third party most likely provided the web beacon?
A. a social media website (correct)
B. the larger brewer wishing to buy the smaller brewer
C. the Federal Trade Commission
D. the Federal Communications Commission
Explanation:
Social media websites make use of web beacons placed on different websites to see what types of websites their users visit. This way they can create advertising profiles of their users, which allows them to sell advertisements in a targeted way. Option A is the correct answer. Important to note here is that the third-party web beacon can only be placed by the owner of the website, so the brewery is partly responsible in this case.

25. When would the Controlling the Assault of Non-Solicited Pornography and Marketing Act most likely require the brewery to include a warning label in its commercial marketing e-mails?
A. if the alcohol percentage of the beer the e-mail pertains to exceeds 6.5% and the beer qualifies as strong liquor
B. if the logo used by the brewery for one of its beers contains a naked person (correct)
C. if it concerns a mass e-mail, not addressed to a specific person
D. if there is no prior business relationship with the addressees
Explanation:
For erotic material, a warning label needs to be included, for which the label with a naked person could qualify. Option B is the correct answer.

A US government agency that deals with policies in North America is cracking down on laziness within the agency. From a recent survey, it became clear that the employees of the agency have a bad reputation, and are considered to be extremely lazy and unfriendly.

To combat the bad image, an advertisement campaign is started, acknowledging the reputation and promising to work hard to change the culture within the agency. Internally, a carrot and stick approach is used. Employees that achieve good results are rewarded with the possibility to attend interesting training and conferences, whereas employees that show incompetence or lethargy are suspended without pay.

The feedback from the survey showed that employees were often away from the desk where citizens were coming for assistance, either on smoke breaks or bathroom breaks. To verify any similar complaints in the future, CCTV cameras are placed outside the restroom and in the smoking area.

Sure enough, a complaint from an angry citizen arrives, and the director of the agency checks the footage of the CCTV cameras. The employee in question is not found to be either smoking or in the restroom for an extended period. However, the director does see two other employees of the opposite sex passionately enter the men's room at the moment he checks the live feed. Without giving it a second thought, he runs in and catches the two employees in the act.

26. If one or more of the employees initiate litigation, which tort is least likely to be used?
A. intrusion upon seclusion
B. unreasonable invasion of property (correct)
C. publicity given to private life
D. defamation
Explanation:
Unreasonable invasion of property is not a tort that would likely be used in this case. Option B is the most correct answer.

27. Before starting employment, a comprehensive overview of the privacy practices, including the use of CCTV, is provided to the employees. Which type of person is most likely not going to read the document?

A. the privacy unconcerned (correct)
B. the privacy pragmatists
C. the privacy liberalists
D. the privacy utilitarian
Explanation:
The privacy unconcerned, like the name suggests, are not too concerned with their privacy. Therefore, they are less likely to read the document with an overview of privacy practices. Option A is the correct answer.

28. Which type of risk is least present in the workplace at this government agency?
A. reputational risk
B. investment risk (correct)
C. organizational risk
D. legal risk
Explanation:
There is less likely to be an investment risk since it concerns a government agency, which generally has less to do with investments than an organization in the private sector. The other three risks are more likely to be present. Option B is the correct answer.

29. In case the agency uses a contractor to maintain and operate the CCTV cameras, which of the following is most likely true?
A. the contractor is responsible for creating an inventory of laws the agency is required to comply with, and adapt their practices
B. the agency needs to assure that the contractor is compliant with the agency's privacy policy (correct)
C. the contractor is required to hire a privacy officer
D. the agency's privacy officer is required to approve the installing of CCTV cameras
Explanation:
It is the responsibility of the organization that hires a third party to ensure the required level of privacy is maintained. In practice this can mean taking steps to make sure a third party is aware of the required level of privacy and has a contractual incentive to provide it. Option B is the correct answer.

30. When the CCTV cameras are filming inconsistently due to a malfunction, which of the following is most likely affected?
A. confidentiality
B. integrity (correct)
C. availability
D. distribution
Explanation:
The integrity of the information cannot be assured, since filming only parts of an event could create an incorrect impression. Think of a fight between employees where the first punch is not captured on film. Option B is the correct answer.

Donald is a middle-aged US citizen that worked a mediocre job all his life and almost fully paid off his student debt. He has never missed a payment or gotten into financial trouble in any other way and decided not to spend more money than absolutely necessary until he has paid off his student debt in full.

One day, he finds his dream job. He truly feels the universe is rewarding him for his years of hard work. However, the company performs a background check after Donald is hired. The background check results in quite a bit of dirt and the company informs Donald that it has changed its mind.

Furiously Donald asks the company to explain further. The company explains that the background check shows Donald went bankrupt before and has made some terrible investments in the hotel sector. Donald informs them this is false, and that it must be a different Donald, but the company trusts the report it received from the Consumer Reporting Agency over Donald's word.

Donald's previous employer hears about what happened and offers to take Donald back on the condition that he undergoes a polygraph test to verify that nothing of concern to them has happened. Happy to return to work, Donald agrees. During the polygraph test the question regarding diseases in the family comes up, and the employer finds out Donald has an above-average risk to get early-onset Alzheimer's. He is not rehired, ends up on the street, and passes away shortly after.

31. Which of the following, besides the Federal Trade Commission and Federal Communications Commission, is most likely concerned with Donald's privacy in this scenario?
A. the Department of Education
B. the Department of Health Services
C. the Office of Legislative Affairs
D. the Equal Employment Opportunity Commission (correct)
Explanation:
Of the mentioned options, option D is least unlikely given that the case concerns employment.

32. If Donald wishes to litigate, when can he start?
A. if the background check was performed without a permissible purpose (correct)
B. if not performed for evaluating his candidacy
C. if he has not approved the performance of a background check
D. if the background check goes back to his high school years
Explanation:
Before performing a background check, the company must have a permissible purpose. Option A is the most correct answer. Some of the other options may also be (partially) correct, but the earliest correct step mentioned is option A.

33. If Donald's bankruptcy were indeed real, where could he possibly find a source of privacy protection?
A. the Bankruptcy Act (correct)
B. the Equal Employment Opportunity Commission
C. the Inmate Rehabilitation Act
D. the Fair and Accurate Credit Transactions Act
Explanation:
There is such a thing called the Bankruptcy Act, which prohibits discrimination against persons that filed for bankruptcy in the employment process. Option A is the correct answer.

34. Before obtaining a consumer report from a Consumer Reporting Agency, what must the company have done according to Section 604(f) of the Fair Credit Reporting Act?
A. notified Donald that adverse action might be taken
B. disclosed to Donald that the company will obtain a consumer report
C. certified that the consumer report will be used for permissible purposes (correct)
D. informed Donald of his right to receive a free copy of his credit score annually
Explanation:
It must be certified, before receiving a consumer report, that the consumer report will only be used for permissible purposes. Option C is the correct answer.

35. If, as a compromise, the company that rejected Donald offers to let him take a lie detector test to correct their information. Which of the following is most likely true?

A. the company is not allowed to use the results Donald offers of a lie detector test he administered at an independent agency (correct)

B. the company is only allowed to administer a psychological stress test

C. the company is only allowed to administer a polygraph test

D. the company is only allowed to administer a voice stress test

Explanation:

See the Employee Polygraph Protection Act. No lie detector test results are allowed to be used. Option A is the correct answer. The other options are all a type of lie detector test.

An application that can be installed on cell phones called *Cycle-Chat* allows those going for long bicycle rides to connect to those at home who would like to enjoy the view of the bicycle tour. In return, those enjoying the view at home are requested to cheer the cyclist on at the times when the cycling gets tough.

The cell phone is placed in a small contraption on the cyclist's bicycle. This contraption allows those connected with the phone of the cyclist to turn the camera of the phone to the view they wish to see. The idea is that it is a non-recorded session, and there is an incentive for users to return rather than re-watch a previously recorded bicycle ride.

Cycle-Chat turns out to be a great success. It has thousands of users, especially in mountain areas. One of its positive effects is that it allows the users at home to inform the emergency services in case the cyclist falls. This has encouraged a large number of lonely cyclists to become more active and wipe the dust off their old racing bicycles.

However, at the peak of its success, hackers gained access to the passwords of all users. These were stored without any hashing. In addition, it turned out that through a third-party patch on the application, users were able to store the entire exchange, unlike what was promulgated in Cycle-Chat's privacy statement.

36. What does it mean that Cycle-Chat stored passwords without hashing them?
A. only a 256-bit decryption device was needed to open the password file
B. the firewall could easily be bypassed to reach the passwords
C. the passwords were improperly compressed
D. the passwords were directly readable without any decoding (correct)
Explanation:
Hashing ensures that passwords are not readily readable and that an algorithm is needed to decipher them. This can be explained in a more complex way, but for the exam you will likely not have to go deeper than this. Option D is the correct answer.

37. In case Cycle-Chat stores the video streams to later develop a biking video usable for home trainers, which of the following is likely true?

A. storing the video streams is a deceptive trade practice, as this is the opposite of what was communicated to the users (correct)

B. if the streams are de-identified before sending them to the contractor that develops the video collection for home trainers, there is no issue

C. the users are required to be informed afterward and should be presented with a choice on any future capturing of their video streams

D. given that the privacy notice is allowed to be changed at any moment, Cycle-Chat has the freedom to process personal information in any way it desires

Explanation:
A deceptive trade practice is a practice where the actual practice differs from the communicated practice. Option A is the correct answer.

38. Given the similarities to the SnapChat case, what will likely happen?

A. a consent decree will be issued, where Cycle-Chat admits guilt and promises improvement

B. there will be no consequences for Cycle-Chat, as it is a powerless victim of hacking

C. the security officer will be replaced as a consequence of Federal Trade Commission intervention

D. a consent order for not engaging in these business practices for 20 years will be entered into (correct)

Explanation:
Option D is what the SnapChat case resulted in, and therefore the correct answer. When studying the cases in your study materials, try to see the logic of the decisions and figure out the reasons why the Federal Trade Commission took action.

39. If the breach were required to be communicated, at which point would this most likely have been the case?
A. at the most expeditious time and without unreasonable delay (correct)
B. as soon as possible
C. immediately after the final investigation is concluded
D. five business days after the breach was identified
Explanation:
The definition "at the most expeditious time and without unreasonable delay" is a phrase that is commonly used. Option A is the correct answer, the others are too vague, arbitrary, or leave an organization too much freedom to stretch the deadline.

40. If the hack occurred in 2003, in which state would the consequences for Cycle-Chat most likely be highest?
A. New York
B. California (correct)
C. Ohio
D. Florida
Explanation:
California had the first data breach law in 2003, option B is the correct answer. If you are presented a list of states, and you are not sure what the correct answer is, California might be your best chance.

A company called *Medical4all* supplies homeopathic medication, which can be ordered directly on its website without any prescription. The homeopathic medication in its catalog consists of every piece of alternative medication imaginable, whether proven to work or not. In addition, it covers some conventional over-the-counter medicine that is at times covered by their customers' medical insurance.

Recently you have been hired by the company as a security and privacy officer. You are helping the company to both fend off attacks from those hacktivists aggressively opposing the spread of homeopathic medication because they claim it prevents people from seeking the medical care they need, as well as advising the company on how to deal with the large amount of sensitive data it handles.

At some point, you figure out that a few weeks before you started working for the company, there was an unauthorized access to a large amount of customer data. One consequence was that the purchase histories could be viewed. The logs reveal that within a short period, over 75% of the customer files have been accessed, and it cannot be excluded that a copy was made.

The CEO of the website is not worried. She even reveals that they sell a list of customers to a pharmaceutical marketing agency, which uses it to deliver targeted advertisements through social media.

41. Under which law will it most likely be required to report the breach?
A. the Health Information Technology for Economic and Clinical Health Act (correct)
B. the Health Insurance Portability and Accountability Act
C. the Children's Online Privacy Protection Act
D. the Health Care Data Breach Act
Explanation:
The Health Information Technology for Economic and Clinical Health Act contains a breach notification requirement for Personal Health Information. Option A is the correct answer.

42. If the website also targets citizens in the European Union, what would the biggest objection against selling a list of customers to a marketing agency be?

A. the Data Protection Authority in Europe would be able to conduct an investigation

B. consent from part of the individuals on the list would be required (correct)

C. a data processing agreement would be required before selling the list

D. the company would liable for what third parties do with the list

Explanation:

For citizens of the European Union, consent is required before processing sensitive personal data. In this scenario, information about health is highly likely to qualify as sensitive personal data, resulting in the requirement to ask each individual for consent. Option B is correct.

43. Which of the following best describes the selling of a list of customers to a marketing agency?

A. an unfair trade practice

B. a data breach

C. a deceptive trade practice (correct)

D. a security incident

Explanation:

The selling of data is likely not mentioned in the privacy notice, and doing so while having created a different impression could be considered a deceptive trade practice. Option C is the correct answer.

44. The website collects IP addresses. When is an IP address most likely to be considered personal information?

A. when it is dynamic

B. when the IP address is from a country in the European Union

C. when it is static (correct)

D. when the IP address is from the US

Explanation:

Static IP addresses do not change, meaning it is assigned to one internet connection, resulting in all actions performed over that internet connection being linked to it (which is potentially revealing). Option C is the correct answer.

45. A customer file consists of the customer's name, purchase history, IP address, web activity, and shipping address. Which of the elements need to be removed to ensure the customer file is not personal information anymore?
A. customer name
B. customer name, IP address, shipping address
C. customer name, IP address, web activity, and shipping address (correct)
D. customer name, shipping address
Explanation:
Option C is the only option that removes sufficient elements to ensure that the data cannot be traced back to an individual. Option C is the correct answer.

A large international banking corporation based in the US, which offers services to both individuals and companies. The corporation has a large customer base. It has millions of clients globally and as a result processes millions of transactions on a daily basis.

Recently interest rates have dropped, and so has the banking corporation's profit. To compensate for this, the banking corporation started creating profiles of clients, based on the transactions that customers perform. For example, if several transactions in a sporting goods store show up, it is added to that person's profile that the person is interested in sports. If several transactions in a short period of time in a baby clothes shop show up, a label of *parent* is added to that person's profile.

Based on these transactions, targeted advertisement is shown to the clients. This occurs through the advertisement space on the banking corporation's website being sold based on the profiles of its users. If a person classified as being into sports logs in, within a millisecond, a signal is sent to the advertisement provider, and a sports-related advertisement is displayed.

The targeted advertisement proves to be quite lucrative, and the banking corporation decides to take it to the next level. Lists of phone numbers, addresses, and e-mail addresses are sold to whoever is interested, including the profile attached to each individual.

46. If, based on the profiles created by the bank, hackers target an individual and send e-mails tailored to that person, with malicious software to gain entry to that individual's bank account, what would this be called?
A. spam
B. social engineering
C. spear phishing (correct)
D. unauthorized access
Explanation:
Spear phishing is the targeting of one particular individual. Option C is the correct answer. Option B could also be applicable under certain conditions but is a more general term for techniques used to manipulate individuals by exploiting their weaknesses.

47. If, in addition to digital advertising, the bank starts calling customers, which of the following will least likely reduce the bank's liability in case something goes wrong?
A. a written procedure about not calling unwanted
B. trained personnel
C. a data inventory (correct)
D. a Do Not Call list specifically for the bank
Explanation:
A data inventory does very little as regards showing compliance with the applicable telemarketing rules because it only results in an overview of personal information types the company processes. Option C is the correct answer.

48. The bank sells the list to a company but misspelled the addressee's e-mail address. What type of data breach is this most likely?
A. unintended disclosure (correct)
B. physical loss
C. insider
D. hacking or malware
Explanation:
Unintended disclosure is the only one of the options applicable because the list is sent to a different recipient than intended. Option A is the correct answer.

49. In this scenario, the practices most likely violate which of the following rights from the Consumer Privacy Bill of Rights?
A. access and accuracy
B. security
C. purpose limitation
D. respect for context (correct)
Explanation:
A customer will likely not expect that his transactions are processed further beyond being recorded. Option D is the correct answer.

50. From a General Data Protection Regulation perspective, what role does the bank most likely have at the moment it is selling lists of contact data?

A. a processor
B. a business associate
C. a third party
D. a controller (correct)

Explanation:

The bank is a controller because it determines the means and purposes of the data processing. Option D is the correct answer.

Organizations often use software to create an overview of their data processing, types of data they collect, classifications, data breaches, and other privacy or security-related information. Software packages for this purpose are widely available, and given the large number of providers of such software packages, they are relatively cheap.

You work for a company that sells domain names. There is really not much to it, except recording where a visitor is supposed to be guided to when a certain domain name is entered into a web browser. The list of customers is not stored on a server connected to the internet, only on a local server to which the building has access.

Given the recent privacy and security trend, and the developments in legislation, your company has purchased an online software package called *Privacy Safe*. An inventory of all processes is created using the software, as well as a label of the category of data, after which the software indicates which laws are applicable and what the possible restrictions are. In addition, in case of a data breach, this can be recorded using the software, and a report with action points will be generated.

Then, ironically, the company that sells Privacy Safe was the victim of a cyber-attack. All data were accessed, including the databases of the company's customers. This means the data you entered in the software for your organization were also accessed.

51. In which case is a data inventory as described in this scenario likely mandatory?
A. if an institution is covered by the Family Educational Rights and Privacy Act
B. in case the organization transfers personal information to Canadian government institutions
C. if the Chief Information Security Officer has deemed the inventory mandatory
D. if an institution is covered by the Gramm-Leach-Bliley Act (correct)
Explanation:
Under the Gramm-Leach-Bliley Act, a data inventory can be required for an organization. Option D is the correct answer.

52. The Privacy Safe software did not encrypt the data properly. Which case is this similar to?

A. Lifelock Inc. (correct)

B. Vulcan

C. Geocities Inc.

D. Nomi

Explanation:

Lifelock Inc. did not properly encrypt its data, similar to this scenario. Option A is the correct answer.

53. If the Privacy Safe software contains an HTML part containing a pixel that registers the IP address that loads each time the software is started, what would that be called?

A. a log pixel

B. a monitoring pixel

C. a web beacon (correct)

D. user tracking file

Explanation:

A web beacon is a transparent pixel that is loaded, through which it can be logged that the pixel is loaded and from where. Option C is the correct answer. The other options sound similar, but web beacon is the conventional term for it, which you should be aware of as a privacy professional.

54. Which of the following will least likely be considered processing of personal information?

A. keeping a file containing categories of personal information (correct)

B. printing a list of e-mail addresses

C. logging the access of wireless devices on the network

D. requiring the scan of a badge where access rights are granted to employees' badge number

Explanation:

Keeping a file of categories of personal information is not actually keeping Personal Information (only the names of the categories). Option A is the correct answer, the other options all likely contain Personal Information.

55. If the company wants to share its cyber threat indicators, what is required first?
A. the removal of identifiers (correct)
B. permission from those involved
C. Federal Trade Commission approval
D. Federal Communications Commission approval
Explanation:
The removal of identifiers is required before sharing. Option A is the correct answer. If you are not aware of the requirement, the correct answer can also be guessed, as removing identifiers de-identifies the data, meaning the level of required protection will likely go down.

The Federal Bureau of Investigation is investigating a person suspected of hatching terrorist plans. An anonymous tip was sent to the Federal Bureau of Investigation by a concerned citizen who attends the same religious gatherings as the suspect. The anonymous tip contains the information that the suspect takes the religious texts that are provided to him literally, and is unable to place them in a modern-day context. The suspect recently acquired several weapons, legally.

According to the Federal Bureau of Investigation's records, the suspect indeed purchased two weapons recently, which can cause a lot of damage if used inappropriately. This in itself is not unusual, but combined with the tip from the anonymous person they consider there to be sufficient reason to place a wiretap and intercept the suspect's e-mail exchange.

You are an employee of the internet provider of the suspect and have been requested by the Federal Bureau of Investigation to assist in the interception of his e-mails. Since the e-mail uses the encryption your company has implemented, the Federal Bureau of Investigation needs your help to decipher the intercepted data.

At first you are reluctant, because the Federal Bureau of Investigation does not share any information as to why the suspect is under investigation. In addition, you find out that the suspect was a citizen of the EU prior to becoming a US citizen, and there could be some applicable restrictions following from the General Data Protection Regulation.

56. When shipping the discovered evidence on a physical medium, which of the following would you consider most important from a legal point of view?
A. shipping on Solid State Drives
B. shipping in a way that preserves an audit trail (correct)
C. shipping with adequately protected backups
D. shipping files with 256-bit encryption
Explanation:
An audit trail can ensure that it is visible who accessed or modified the files. This can be important. The other options add to the security. Option B is the correct answer.

57. If the data of the suspect are stored largely in Europe, which of the following might provide restrictions regarding the access to the data?

A. the Personal Information Protection and Electronic Documents Act

B. the General Data Protection Regulation (correct)

C. the Protection of Personal Information Act

D. the CLOUD Act

Explanation:

The General Data Protection Regulation also applies to citizens from outside of the European Union whose data are processed in the European Union. Option B is the correct answer. Option A is applicable to Canada, option C is applicable to South Africa and option D would make the process easier.

58. If in the privacy notice, your company has promised its clients not to share their personal information with third parties, including law enforcement, what could happen if you do provide access to the Federal Bureau of Investigation?

A. section 5 of the Federal Trade Commission Act could be enforced (correct)

B. the evidence gathered is inadmissible in court

C. an automatic fine is triggered

D. the client has the authority to call the gathering of evidence to a halt

Explanation:

It could be a deceptive trade practice, for which section 5 of the Federal Trade Commission Act is relevant. Option A is the correct answer.

59. Under the computer trespasser exception, if applicable, which of the following statement is most appropriate?
A. you are obliged to cooperate
B. you are not allowed to cooperate without a warrant
C. you are not allowed to provide instruction but are allowed to provide access
D. you are free to cooperate, as well as free to refuse cooperation (correct)
Explanation:
The computer trespasser exception allows you to cooperate but does not make it mandatory. Option D is the correct answer.

60. If the Federal Bureau of Investigation wants to intercept the e-mail of the suspect, what is generally required?
A. a subpoena
B. a warrant
C. a court order or other lawful basis (correct)
D. encryption
Explanation:
A court order is likely required. Option C is the correct answer.

A gigantic marketing campaign has been launched for a new electric toothbrush. People are encouraged to take part in a lottery, for which they have to fill out a form with a few questions. Those with the correct answers are entered into the lottery, with a vacation to Paris for the winner and a few electric toothbrushes to be given away to a few less lucky contestants.

When entering the lottery, a notice is provided that states that your personal information will be used to make this lottery possible. The example regarding your address is mentioned, as in that the company needs your address to ship your prize in case you win. This makes it seem as if the marketing campaign stops after the lottery.

However, long after the lottery ended, the list with personal information on all contestants is still kept by the company. The company intends to use it in case there are other marketing campaigns, although this was not indicated in the notice provided to people when signing up for the lottery.

The toothbrush company is doing well, after which the CEO decides to sell it. Its technology and customer service department are bought by a competitor. This competitor is mostly interested in the technology that was embedded in the toothbrush because it has the ability to change programming based on the user's brushing habits.

61. The toothbrush connects to open WIFI connections if it detects them, and transmits data about the frequency of its use to the manufacturer. What can be said about the data transmitted to the manufacturer?
A. the amount of use of a toothbrush is personal information
B. no permission is required from the user
C. this could be considered sensitive personal data in Europe, depending on the other data a manufacturer can link to that specific device (correct)
D. a notice informing the user of the connection to WIFI is not required, as it does not transmit anything about the user, only about the device
Explanation:
If the manufacturer can link the toothbrush to a specific person, and the brushing habits reveal something about that person's health, it could be considered sensitive personal data. Option C is correct.

62. Which of the following is in line with the purposes identified in the notice?
A. storing the personal information (correct)
B. selling the personal information
C. re-using the personal information
D. using the personal information for marketing purposes
Explanation:
Storing personal information is required for the lottery, hence in line with the privacy notice. Option A is correct. The other options are not required for the lottery.

63. If the toothbrush connects to WIFI, what is this type of phenomenon commonly referred to?
A. device enabled Personal Information sharing
B. human-device exposure
C. Virtual Reality
D. the Internet of Things (correct)
Explanation:
The Internet of Things describes the phenomenon of physical devices connected with each other over the internet, which is applicable to this case. Option D is correct.

64. If the toothbrush company enters into a consent decree with the Federal Trade Commission, which of the following is most likely true?
A. the Federal Trade Commission has one-sidedly forced the company to pay a fine
B. a judge ordered the illegal activity to come to a halt, and for the company to pay a fine in case it violates the consent decree
C. the company committed unfair and deceptive practices
D. it agrees to stop the alleged wrong activity without admitting wrongdoing (correct)
Explanation:
A consent decree generally involves agreeing to stop something without admitting wrongdoing. Option D is correct.

65. If the toothbrush company has entered into a consent decree regarding its privacy practices, and seemingly violates that consent decree, what is most likely to happen?
A. a Federal Trade Commission investigation (correct)
B. enforcement in the Federal District court
C. civil penalties
D. injunctions
Explanation:
If a violation (allegedly) takes place, there will first be an investigation before any other steps are taken. Option A is correct.

After going through a tough period, having taken many wrong turns, your life is slowly starting to get back on track. You have battled with drug addiction for years, and after treatment in a well-known clinic, you have completely kicked the habit.

You get back to your old life, and your family, friends, and colleagues understand your situation and give you all the support you need. In addition, you attend a support group every two weeks, where you discuss your experiences with those who share the same fate to some extent.

All is going well, and you stay clean. Your doctor prescribes you tablets that help you with keeping the urges away, which are fully covered by your health insurance. Obviously, you accept all the help you can get, and diligently use the medication as prescribed.

One day, your spouse sits you down and looks at you angrily. It turns out a pharmaceutical company has phoned, asking your oldest child how the withdrawal symptoms are and whether they can send you their newest medication. Your child now knows you had a drug problem.

66. When will the clinic least likely be subject to the Health Insurance Portability and Accountability Act for your treatment?
A. if you pay in cash out of your own pocket (correct)
B. if one of the privacy rule exemptions applies
C. if the program receives federal funding
D. if the clinic is run by volunteers
Explanation:
If no electronic transactions take place and no insurance claim is filed, the Health Insurance Portability and Accountability Act will likely not apply. Option A is the correct answer.

67. The clinic wants to sell the information subject to the Drug Abuse, Prevention, Treatment and Rehabilitation Act. What would most likely allow this?
A. a legitimate interest
B. the patient's written consent (correct)
C. a court order
D. a subpoena
Explanation:
If a patient provides written consent, this leaves more room for disclosure. Option B is the most correct answer.

68. Which of the following fits the definition of patient-identifying information best, in the context of the clinic?
A. any information that can directly or indirectly identify a person diagnosed with substance abuse (correct)
B. any information related to a natural person
C. any information regarding the type of drug a person abused
D. the status of the patient in his or her rehabilitation process
Explanation:
A is the correct answer. The other options are also somewhat correct, but less complete and less specific than option A. If you are doubting between answers on the exam, it can be useful to check how complete and specific the options are and decide based on that.

69. If the pharmaceutical company has received your name on a list which it bought from the clinic, which case would this be similar to?
A. Eli Lilly & Co
B. TRENDnet Inc.
C. Geocities Inc. (correct)
D. DesignerWare LLC
Explanation:
In the case of Geocities Inc., personal information was sold. Option C is the correct answer.

70. If the treatment clinic received federal funding for the program you took part in, which of the following can least likely be done with your Personal Information?

A. use the information in a way that can lead to criminal charges against the patient (correct)

B. use the information in a way that can lead to criminal charges

C. use your written information

D. use your verbally provided information

Explanation:

The Drug Abuse Prevention, Treatment and Rehabilitation Act applies when federal funding is received and restricts the use of information that can lead to criminal charges concerning alcohol or drug use.

One afternoon you arrive home from work early and hear the door closing in the back of the house. You cautiously explore the house and find your wife on the couch in lingerie. When you ask her who just left and why she is wearing lingerie, she says she just entered the house and was waiting in the backyard to see you arrive and surprise you.

After foolishly believing your wife and having a wonderful afternoon, doubt starts to kick in. You cannot grasp why she would wait for you in the backyard rather than just observe through the window. She must be unfaithful to you. You decide to hire a private investigator to find out more.

The private investigator comes back with the news that your wife is indeed cheating on you. In fact, she even seduced the private investigator, which he shows you on the footage of the hidden camera he placed in his van where your wife followed him to.

Immediately you want to file for divorce. However, you want to approach things with caution, to make sure your wife gets the least possible in the divorce. You are not sure to which extent the evidence you have gathered is legal and allowed to be used.

71. If your wife's lawyer sends you a request to hand over the records the private investigator created of her, which form would that request most likely be in?
A. a subpoena (correct)
B. a warrant
C. a national security letter
D. a compliance note
Explanation:
A subpoena is the most likely in this case. Option A is the correct answer.

72. When your wife requests the fact that it was her birthday the day she cheated on you with the private investigator be left out of the information provided during e-discovery, what is this most likely called?
A. redaction (correct)
B. restriction
C. legal editing
D. relevance testing
Explanation:
Redaction means leaving out certain pieces of information, such as the date of birth. Option A is the most correct answer.

73. In case the court is not covered by the Federal Rules of Civil Procedure, and your wife wishes the medical information supporting her case supplied by her health insurance not to be made public, which of the following can most likely provide help?
A. a qualified protective order (correct)
B. the Health Information Technology for Economic and Clinical Health Act disclosure restriction
C. an extended Federal Rules of Civil Procedure application
D. the Fourth Amendment
Explanation:
Under the Health Insurance Portability and Accountability Act, this would be called a qualified protective order. Option A is the correct answer.

74. If the court orders the information revealed about the behavior of your wife not to be disclosed outside the courtroom, what would this most likely be referred to?
A. information restriction
B. e-discovery limitation
C. protective order (correct)
D. the Fourth Amendment right to prevent unreasonable disclosure
Explanation:
A protective order can prohibit disclosure of Personal Information that was revealed during litigation. Option C is the correct answer.

75. If your wife is served a subpoena, but does not obey, what is most likely going to happen?
A. forfeiture of the court case
B. a fine or prison (correct)
C. she will be excluded from the e-discovery process
D. a new date for the court case will have to be established
Explanation:
Disobeying a subpoena can lead to a fine or time in prison. Option B is the correct answer.

A small bakery started a surprise bread service tit calls *bread of the world*, where the bakery bakes different types of bread and delivers them to its customers. Of course, the point of the bread service is to taste different kinds of bread, so the bakery decided that its customers buy a subscription after which the bread is delivered.

In order not to cause any health issues, customers are requested to fill out a form indicating any food-related allergies they have. This way, with the variety of bread styles, a customer will not receive the weekly bread if it contains any of the dangerous allergens.

A database with all customers, their allergies, and their credit card numbers is stored on the local computer in the bakery. The computer is connected to the internet since a large part of the bakery's customers order through the bakery's website.

One day, the owner turns on the computer and sees a message displayed on the screen, stating that a certain amount of cryptocurrency needs to be paid to unlock the computer. It turns out, a malicious file was opened and the computer got infected with malware. The owner picks up his computer and smashes it, hoping to solve the problem this way.

76. If the bakery were located in the European Union, what could provide an issue?
A. consent would be required for all processing of personal data
B. the Health Insurance Portability and Accountability Act applies to allergy information
C. the allergy information could be considered sensitive personal data (correct)
D. the Data Protection Authority needs to be informed of the processing
Explanation:
The allergy information reveals something about a person's health, which is sensitive personal data. In this scenario, this would require all persons that submit allergy information to provide valid consent for the use of the data. Option C is the correct answer.

77. Which of the following would result in the most secure storage of the sensitive files the bakery processes, such as allergy information and financial information?
A. using a firewall
B. compressing the files to make them more difficult for hackers to find
C. scanning for viruses regularly
D. using encryption and storing the data offline (correct)
Explanation:
If something is stored offline, it is difficult to access from a distance, reducing the risk of unauthorized access significantly. Combined with encryption, this provides the best option. Option D is the correct answer.

78. Which of the following would least likely be considered a transactional or relationship message?
A. an e-mail to confirm an order
B. an e-mail to inform about a change in the delivery schedule
C. an e-mail to inform the customer that it can return the bread of last week and receive a refund
D. an e-mail to potential customers that have been suggested by existing customers (correct)
Explanation:
An e-mail to persons that no prior business relationship exists with is the riskiest of the mentioned options. Option D is the correct answer.

79. One day the bakery chats with a customer, explaining it is preparing the bread baskets for the diabetic customers. On one of the baskets, the customer sees the name of one of the applicants for the job she is conducting interviews for next week. What will most likely prevent her from doing anything with the information?

A. the Genetic Information and Nondiscrimination Act (correct)

B. the Health Insurance Portability and Accountability Act

C. the Health Information Technology for Economic and Clinical Health Act

D. the state data breach legislation

Explanation:

The Genetic Information and Nondiscrimination Act forbids discrimination based on what the customer has seen (such as the fact that the applicant has diabetes, which could indicate an employee needing time for medical care). Option A is the correct answer.

80. In case the bakery provides a notice of what the bakery will do with your data and the services it delivers, after which you decide to share your personal information, what needs to be present for the privacy notice to be considered a contract?

A. both parties agreeing to the terms

B. terms for changing the practices

C. an offer, acceptance, and consideration (correct)

D. a third reviewing party

Explanation:

An offer, acceptance, and consideration are required for something to be a contract. Option C is the correct answer.

A hotel chain has recently been involved in a scandal. One staff member was upset over the low salary and the hotel's policy of collecting all tips and distributing them evenly over the staff. To get revenge, she placed cameras in the rooms of the hotel guests.

The disgruntled employee also had access to the guest registry. Access to the live streams was sold on the dark web. The live streams of high-profile hotel guests resulted in the highest price. It took several years for the practice to be discovered by law enforcement, and happened after a guest was sent images of himself with his mistress.

To add to the scandal, someone who considered himself a cyber vigilante made an anonymous phone call to the police anytime a crime showed up on the live stream. This included anything without consent.

Finally, when a politician was discovered with an underaged child, someone watching the live stream intervened and broke into the hotel room to save the child. The whole live stream was recorded and sent to the police as evidence. This resulted in the hidden camera practice being uncovered.

81. What would have most significantly lowered the chances of this incident occurring?
A. frequent audits on the WIFI network
B. forbidding Virtual Private Network connection over the WIFI servers
C. providing the personnel with security training (correct)
D. appointing a Chief Information Security Officer
Explanation:
If the personnel is provided with security training, they would be made aware of similar scenarios and be aware of a camera or other device that should not be present. The other options tackle the problem less efficiently. Option C is the correct answer.

82. If the video stream cannot be traced back to the hotel, which of the following is most untrue?
A. there is a significant invasion of privacy
B. it does not matter whether the location is known, the chance of the person on the video being identified results in it containing personal information
C. the level of responsibility of the hotel depends, to an extent, on which controls it has in place to prevent these types of incidents
D. the video stream no longer contains personal information (correct)
Explanation:
The issue here is whether the persons in the video are identifiable. Whether or not the video can be traced back to the hotel has little effect if the persons in the video are identifiable. Option D is the correct answer, as the video stream still contains personal information if the guests are identifiable.

83. In case the perpetrator installed wireless devices that connected with a cell phone tower to transmit the video stream, which of the following is the most likely to reveal the source of the perpetrator?
A. the telecom company (correct)
B. the hotel's human resources department
C. the perpetrator
D. the users of the video stream
Explanation:
The telecom company is the one who should have the most information about the owner of the device (unless it is stolen and the theft went unnoticed). Option A is the correct answer, and the other options likely either do not know or will not share the source of the perpetrator.

84. The security officer has detected a stream of data that could not be read. What is most likely the case?

A. the stream was sent over a Virtual Private Network connection (correct)

B. the compression was unable to keep up

C. unsupported formats were used

D. the codec of the video steam was uniquely hashed

Explanation:

When connecting to a Virtual Private Network, the data are sent to that network encrypted and unreadable for those without the encryption key. Option A is the correct answer.

85. To which of the following cases is this case similar?

A. Lifelock Inc.

B. TRENDnet

C. Designerware LLC (correct)

D. Vulcan

Explanation:

In the Designerware LLC case, the customers were unaware that the company could provide itself with access to the keystrokes and camera images of its customers. Option C is the correct answer.

A small company has hired you to grow its sales team. You sell car insurance. It is what you have done your entire professional life, and it is what you are good at. Part of your tasks is to make cold calls and convince people to take out insurance or switch to the company's insurance policy.

Every morning you are provided with a list of names and phone numbers. The goal is to call all these numbers that day. Your phone log will be reviewed by the manager at the end of the week, and if the log does not correspond to the numbers on the list you have been provided with, there is a clarification meeting in which a justification needs to be provided.

You also receive a list of e-mails. This list has been obtained from a data broker, who tricked people into providing their personal details in order to win a non-existing prize. It is a large list, but all persons on the list have been categorized by the data broker as owning one or more vehicles.

Before starting work, your colleagues tell you that the e-mails you send are read by the manager. Not only your work e-mail but also the personal messages sent over the company's network. You are not quite sure how this is done, but it may have something to do with the staff application you were obliged to install on your phone before being allowed to commence work.

86. If the data broker gathered his data from public sources, which of the following APEC principles is least relevant?
A. Security safeguards
B. Accountability
C. Choice (correct)
D. Preventing harm
Explanation:
If data are public, choice is less relevant. Option C is the correct answer.

87. If the data broker performed an internet sweep through several sources of public data, which of the following APEC principles is most likely not respected?

A. Accountability

B. Collection limitation (correct)

C. Security safeguards

D. Access and correction

Explanation:

The collection limitation means collection should be limited to the purposes. Since the data broker does not know the purposes of its customers, it has likely collected more than needed for the purposes (excluding his own purpose). Option B is the most correct answer.

88. The company's sales practices are most likely impacted by which of the following?

A. strict state law

B. the Fourth amendment

C. the Controlling the Assault of Non-Solicited Pornography and Marketing Act (correct)

D. the Children's Online Privacy Protection Act

Explanation:

The e-mailing of persons with whom the company does not have a prior business relationship will most likely be subject to restrictions of the Controlling the Assault of Non-Solicited Pornography and Marketing Act. Option C is the correct answer.

89. If the company allows employees to use their own laptops and smartphones to perform their work, which of the following could likely provide the most privacy protection?
A. state law
B. a Bring Your Own Device Policy signed by both parties (correct)
C. an employment manual
D. national law
Explanation:
If the practices are clear and have been made clear to the employee through a policy specifically for the use of personal devices, it is likely to provide the most clarity and the fewest issues. Option B is the correct answer.

90. If the company ignores the Do Not Call registry when contacting someone, what would you hope as a privacy officer to be the case?
A. the calls take place outside of the restricted hours
B. the calls take place within business hours
C. only authorized robocalls take place
D. an existing relationship within the last 18 months (correct)
Explanation:
If an existing business relationship exists from within the last 18 months, the Do Not Call registry does likely not have to be consulted. Option D is the correct answer.

Printed in France by Amazon
Brétigny-sur-Orge, FR

17552333R00058